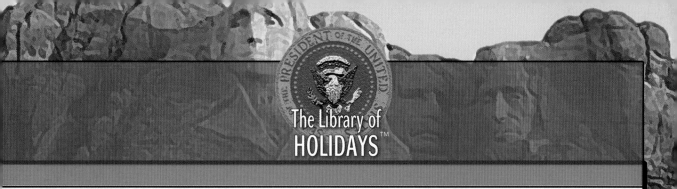

The Library of HOLIDAYS™

Presidents' Day

Amy Margaret

The Rosen Publishing Group's
PowerKids Press™
New York

For Kyeler and Cory

Published in 2002 by The Rosen Publishing Group, Inc.
29 East 21st Street, New York, NY 10010

First Edition

Book Design: Michael Caroleo, Michael de Guzman
Layout: Nick Sciacca
Project Editors: Jennifer Landau, Joanne Randolph

Photo Credits: pp. 4 (Lincoln), 7 (Nixon) © CORBIS; p. 4 (Washington) © Christie's Images/CORBIS; p. 7 © The Corcoran Gallery of Art/CORBIS; pp. 7 (Lincoln), 15, 19 (Roosevelt) © SuperStock; p. 8 © Francis G Mayer/CORBIS; p. 11 © Richard T Norwitz/CORBIS; pp. 12, 19 (Jefferson), 20 © Bettmann/CORBIS; p. 16 © Reuters NewMedia/CORBIS.

Margaret, Amy.
Presidents' Day / by Amy Margaret.— 1st ed.
  p. cm. — (The library of holidays)   4/1/03
Includes bibliographical references and index.
  ISBN 0-8239-5786-1 (lib. bdg.: alk. paper)
1. Presidents' Day—Juvenile literature. 2. Washington, George, 1732–1799—Juvenile literature. 3. Lincoln, Abraham, 1809–1865—Juvenile literature. 4. Presidents—United States—History—Juvenile literature. [1. Presidents' Day. 2. Washington, George, 1732–1799. 3. Lincoln, Abraham, 1809–1865. 4. Presidents. 5. Holidays.] I. Title.
E176.8 .M17 2002
   394.261—dc21
                                                         00–013020

Contents

Presidents' Day

Presidents' Day is a day to celebrate the lives of past U.S. presidents, especially George Washington and Abraham Lincoln. It is observed on the third Monday in February. This day was picked because it falls in between the two men's birthdays. George Washington was born on February 22, 1732, and Abraham Lincoln was born on February 12, 1809. Presidents' Day celebrates **democracy** and the **independence** for which this country fought.

◀ *Presidents' Day celebrates Abraham Lincoln (left), George Washington (right), and all American presidents.*

Presidents' Day was started on February 22, 1796, to celebrate George Washington's birthday. He was America's first president.

On February 12, 1866, many states began celebrating President Abraham Lincoln's birthday. Lincoln had been shot and killed in April 1865. In 1971, President Richard Nixon made the two celebrations one. The third Monday in February would be Presidents' Day. Nixon said this day would honor all past presidents.

President Richard Nixon (bottom right) made the third Monday in February Presidents' Day. This day honors ▶ *Washington, Lincoln, and all past presidents.*

George Washington

George Washington grew up in Virginia. He did not go to college. Instead, he became a soldier in the Virginia **militia**.

In 1775, Washington led the colonial soldiers in the **Revolutionary War**. In 1783, America won its independence from Britain. Washington was ready to go home. Instead, the **Continental Congress** voted for him to become the first U.S. president. He served two four-year terms. In 1799, he died. He was buried at his home, called Mount Vernon.

◀ *George Washington was a great military leader and president.*

The Washington Monument was built to honor the "father of his country," George Washington. It is located in the capital city of the United States, Washington, D.C. The Washington Monument is the tallest building in the area. It is more than 555 feet tall (169.2 meters). Building of the monument began in 1848. Work stopped in 1858, because there wasn't enough money. In 1878, work continued. The monument was opened to the public in 1888.

Fifty flags circle the Washington Monument, shown here. Each flag stands for one of the fifty states. ▶

Abraham Lincoln

Abraham Lincoln was America's sixteenth president. He often was called Honest Abe. He helped end slavery in the United States.

Lincoln and people in the North felt slavery was wrong and should end. The people in the South felt each state should decide for itself. There were other issues, too. The **Civil War** began in 1861.

Lincoln was shot just before the war ended in April 1865. Unfortunately, he didn't live to see the country brought together again.

◀ *President Lincoln, shown in this photograph with Civil War soldiers, worked hard to end slavery.*

The Lincoln Memorial

The Lincoln Memorial also is located in Washington, D.C., and faces the Washington Monument. Building of the memorial began in 1914, and finished in 1922. The memorial is a large **colonnade** with 36 columns. The columns stand for the 36 states that made up the United States in Lincoln's time. Each column is 44 feet (13.4 m) high. Inside the memorial is a large statue of Abraham Lincoln. On either side of the statue are two important speeches that Lincoln gave.

The Lincoln Memorial was built between 1914 and 1922. Inside the memorial is a statue of Abraham Lincoln, our sixteenth president. ▶

The Work of a U.S. President

There have been many U.S. presidents since George Washington and Abraham Lincoln. Part of the president's job has always been to make sure that the laws of the United States are obeyed. The Constitution is a document containing the rules that the government and the people must follow. The president works closely with the government's **judicial** and **legislative** branches to make sure the country runs smoothly. These branches help to make sure the president does a good job.

◀ *George W. Bush, shown here, is the forty-second president of the United States.*

Great American Presidents

Every president tries to make the United States a better place to live. Some presidents' accomplishments stand out from others, though.

The third U.S. president was Thomas Jefferson. He wrote the Declaration of Independence. He also founded the U.S. Patent Office and was an inventor himself.

Franklin Delano Roosevelt was the thirty-second president. He served almost four full terms. He helped the country get through the **Great Depression** and World War II.

Both Thomas Jefferson (left) and Franklin D. Roosevelt (right) accomplished a great deal as president. ▶

Celebrating Presidents' Day

Presidents' Day can be celebrated in many ways. You can visit the Washington Monument and Lincoln Memorial. You also can go to the yearly wreath-laying ceremony at Washington's grave. He is buried at Mount Vernon, Virginia.

You also may visit one of the 13 presidential libraries in the country. Each library is in the birthplace of a president. You can see items that the presidents used at home and work. You also can remember Washington and Lincoln by having a party in their honor.

◀ *This is a picture of Washington's home in Mount Vernon, Virginia.*

The U.S. Presidents

Here is a list of all the U.S. presidents and the years they served in the White House. To make the most of Presidents' Day, research each president and uncover at least one useful thing each man has done for the United States.

George Washington, 1789–1797
John Adams, 1797–1801
Thomas Jefferson, 1801–1809
James Madison, 1809–1817
James Monroe, 1817–1825
John Quincy Adams, 1825–1829
Andrew Jackson, 1829–1837
Martin Van Buren, 1837–1841
William Henry Harrison, 1841
John Tyler, 1841–1845
James Polk, 1845–1849
Zachary Taylor, 1849–1850
Millard Fillmore, 1850–1853
Franklin Pierce, 1853–1857

James Buchanan, 1857–1861
Abraham Lincoln, 1861–1865
Andrew Johnson, 1865–1869
Ulysses S. Grant, 1869–1877
Rutherford B. Hayes, 1877–1881
James A. Garfield, 1881
Chester A. Arthur, 1881–1885
Grover Cleveland, 1885–1889
Benjamin Harrison, 1889–1893
William McKinley, 1897–1901
Theodore Roosevelt, 1901–1909
William Howard Taft, 1909–1913
Woodrow Wilson, 1913–1921
Warren G. Harding, 1921–1923

Calvin Coolidge, 1923–1929
Herbert Hoover, 1929–1933
Franklin Delano Roosevelt, 1933–1945
Harry S. Truman, 1945–1953
Dwight D. Eisenhower, 1953–1961
John F. Kennedy, 1961–1963
Lyndon B. Johnson, 1963–1969
Richard M. Nixon, 1969–1974
Gerald R. Ford, 1974–1977
Jimmy Carter, 1977–1981
Ronald Reagan, 1981–1989
George Bush, 1989–1993
William Jefferson Clinton, 1993–2001
George W. Bush, 2001–

Glossary

Civil War (SIH-vul WOR) The war between the North and South in the United States from 1861 to 1865.

colonnade (kah-luh-NAYD) A series of columns, usually supporting a roof.

Continental Congress (kon-tin-EN-tul KON-gres) A group that acted as a governing body for the 13 colonies in America.

democracy (dih-MAH-kruh-see) A government that holds free elections, is ruled by a majority, and believes all people deserve equal treatment.

Great Depression (GRAYT dih-PREH-shun) A severe economic downturn in the United States and Europe that lasted from 1929 to 1939.

independence (in-dih-PEN-dents) Freedom from the control, support, or help of other people.

judicial (joo-DIH-shel) The branch of government made up of the Supreme Court.

legislative (LEH-jis-lay-tiv) The branch of government that makes laws and collects taxes.

militia (muh-LIH-shuh) A group of people who are trained and ready to fight in an emergency.

Revolutionary War (reh-vuh-LOO-shuh-nayr-ee WOR) The war that American colonists fought from 1775 to 1783 to win independence from England.

Index

Web Sites

To learn more about Presidents' Day, check out these Web sites:
www.cyberspaceplace.com/holidayring/presidentday.htm
www.patriotism.org/presidents_day/